Tales of the Heart

Cricket CM Ostby

PublishAmerica
Baltimore

© 2007 by Cricket CM Ostby.
All rights reserved. No part of this book may be reproduced, stored in a retrieval system or transmitted in any form or by any means without the prior written permission of the publishers, except by a reviewer who may quote brief passages in a review to be printed in a newspaper, magazine or journal.

First printing

All characters in this book are fictitious, and any resemblance to real persons, living or dead, is coincidental.

PublishAmerica has allowed this work to remain exactly as the author intended, verbatim, without editorial input.

ISBN: 1-60441-344-1
PUBLISHED BY PUBLISHAMERICA, LLLP
www.publishamerica.com
Baltimore

Printed in the United States of America

Table of Contents

Up to You	...9
I Will Always Remember	...11
Kiss upon an Angel's Wings	...12
The Dream	...14
Twister	...15
Cricket	...17
The Rose	...18
No More	...19
Broken Wings	...20
Silent	...21
Emotions	...22
Be Thankful	...23
Open	...25
Two Reflections in the Mirror	...26
The Storm	...28
Razorblades 2-Scars	...29
Memories of My Past	...32
Questions	...34
Brick Wall	...35
Now I Lay Me Down to Sleep	...37
Razorblade—The End	...39
Scars	...40
Pain	...41
Innocence Taken	...42
Beneath the Willow Tree	...44
He Thinks He's Just a Friend	...46

Etched by Scars	...49
I Am	...52
Are You Ready	...54
Angels Cry	...55
Guide Me	...56
Our Guide	...57
If I Had Only Given My All	...59
Take It to the Lord in Prayer	...60
Heaven's Gate	...61
In Another Place	...63
Thank You Friend	...65
Wings of an Angel	...66
Life of Failure	...67
The Secret	...68
Broken Angel	...70
Lost Love	...72
Sick and Tired	...73
My Friend Randy	...74
My Friend	...76
Rodeo	...77
Shady	...79
Behind the Wall	...81
Darkness	...83
Nothing	...84
What I Wanted	...86
Control	...88
Said You Loved Me	...90
Always in the Way	...91
Perfect	...92
Web of Deceit	...94
The Brown Bear	...95
Deer	...96

Tick the Chick	...97
A Cat Named Pat	...98
Drowning in My Sorrow	...99
Only Life I Know	...100
As You Sleep	...102
To Take a Stand	...104
Will You	...105
Someone for Me	...106
To Make a Change	...107
Thin Strands	...109
Band-Aid on Your Feelings	...110

Up to You

Hold my hand,
Let us be,
Fly with me.
Why can't you see?

I need your love.
I need your touch.
I need you by my side.
You know how I have tried.

You just make me cry,
And make me want to die.
Is our love a lie?

Why do I even try?
When all I do is ask why,
As I sit here and sigh.

Tell me what I am to do,
as I really have no clue.

Is this the end?
Or will we begin?

Hold my hand,
And be my man.

This is what I ask of you,
Is this too much for you to do?
Will we be,
Or are we through?
I guess my love;
It's up to you.

I Will Always Remember

The light in your eyes,
Like the stars,
In the night sky,
Twinkling bright.

Your smile as warm,
As the midday sun;
Warm your touch upon my skin.

Your kiss as soft,
As a rose petal,
Light with dew.

I will always remember you.
I miss you mom,
And daddy too.
We will meet again,
When my time is through.

I Love You.

Kiss upon an Angel's Wings

Sitting here now,
Next to you,
Laughing and talking,
To you like I use to do.

Now nothing will ever be the same,
As I sit by this slab,
That bares your name.

I remember how you use to say,
We'd be friends forever,
You'd never go away.

But cancer took you away,
As it did my mom that day,

I miss you both so very much,
I long to feel your tender touch.

I don't know why you had to go,
But I like to think God had a plan
For you and mom you know.

As I feel my tears start to swell,
Inside I just want to yell,
That this day my heart has fell.

I know that we shall be together someday,
And you and mom and dad will be there,
To help me along my way.

I will not say Goodbye,
As we will be together,
Someday in the sky.

I send you a kiss,
Upon angels' wings,
And I'll talk to you again,
When next I dream.

The Dream

As I lay sleeping,
You came to me in a dream,
Oh how real you seemed,
You grabbed my waist and held me close,
Looking into my eyes as your hand ran down my thigh,
Softly touching my lips with your tender kiss,
Caressing me with your touch,
By knees becoming weak,
Hungry for your touch,
You caress my breast,
As your mouth searches for the rest,
Soon our bodies melt into one,
We fit like a glove,
As we made love,
Lying in each others arms,
I felt I was safe from harm,
I turn to give you a kiss,
And I wake,
And find this was only a dream,
But oh how real you seemed.

Twister

It comes by day;
It comes by night,
Such a scary sight.

Twisting, turning, spinning,
Around, rampaging through,
Houses and towns.

Removing anything within its
path,
So many have felt
The twister's wrath.

Removing a home here and there
Bits and pieces filling the air.
Destruction too much,
For anyone to bare.

Such devastation left in its wake,
The twister doesn't give,
It only takes.

Cricket

I the cricket,
Fast and quiet,
And jumping over tall grasses,
In the meadow.

I feel the wind
Softly blowing
Each blade.

I hear the crackle
Of the fire
Burning from a house nearby.

I see
The smoke rising.

I play a tune,
Upon my hind legs,
With the sound of a violin,
In an orchestra.

The Rose

I am a rose,
Dew drops glisten,
Like the clear diamond,
Upon my fragrant petals,
In the morning sun.

Silently swaying,
As a child upon,
His swing.

As red
As a ruby.

The yellow bumblebee
Pollinates me,
Like a man,
To a woman.

No More

I used to run away and hide
To hold everything inside
Like a turtle
I'd crawl inside my shell
Wanting to die
To be released from the hell
The words hurt me
Deep down inside
Until there was nothing left
Not even my pride
But not anymore I said
This is the day I don't run away
I took a stand
And I said No More
Your words cannot hurt me
They're just words you see
I found the strength within me
And I was set free.

Broken Wings

Brought down to the ground with out making a
Sound
Broken wings were all that were seen
She gave all she could give
This wasn't the way she wanted to live
No one could see the pain that lies in her eyes
No one saw her die inside
Each time her children cried
She tried to protect us the best she could
Like any loving mother would
She said his angry words didn't mean anything
But yet it hurt just the same
She wore a smile
But it was a disguise
For we saw the tears in her eyes
We know she hides and silently cries
Brought down to the ground with out
Making a sound
Broken wings were all that were seen.

Silent

A home filled with silence
Too frightened to speak
Our spirits too weak
Broken by your angry words
Your voice, is all that is heard
We try to stay away from you
Seems making you angry
Is all we do
Do you feel some kind of power
By making us cower?
Your anger seems to make you blind
As you can't see the pain
You've left behind

Emotions

Tears are falling like the rain
At times you feel you may go insane
Your heart holds so much pain inside
So many emotions you try to hide
Rolling in and out like the tide
There's nothing you can do
But go along for the ride
Feeling so alone inside
No one here to which I can confide
And so again I swallow my pride
And brush the tears aside.

Be Thankful

Open your eyes and see,
What has been created for you and me,
Water, land, flower, trees,
Even the bumble bees,
Everything we could need,
And yet some want more,
Because of greed.
"Hear my Plea"
Look around and really see,
What has been given to thee.
Shout to the world for all the hear,
Look what He has created here,
Hold all these things near and dear,
If you hold Him near,
There is nothing to fear.
His Love for us is so clear.
Be thankful this day,
Praise Him along the way.
Walk in His light,
For in His arms,
He holds us tight,
Every day and every night,
We are always in His sight,

Strive to do what is right.
Shout out loud!!
For all to hear,
He soon will come,
The time is near,
Nothing to fear,
If His words you hold near.

Open

Open your ears and hear me
Not just listen but hear me
Open your eyes and see me
Not just look at me
But really see me
Open your mouth and talk to me
Not at me
But to me
Open your arms and hug me
Not just touch me
Hug me
Open your heart and Love me
Not just like me
But love me
Open your mind and let me in
And not close it and shut me out
Open yourself to me
As I open myself to you
I am here
Don't shut me out
But let me in

Two Reflections in the Mirror

I look at the mirror upon the wall
And this is what I see
Not just one reflection
But two looking back at me
The first reflection is of who I am now
And the second is the one that wants to be
set free

The first is full of pain and hurt
And made to feel like she is dirt

The second is full of joy
And likes to play with toys

The first wants to die inside
As she has been left with no pride

The second wants to live
She has a lot to give

Will these two reflections
Blend into one
Or will the first never be able
To see the sun

Because for her
Life is already done.
She has no where left
To run

I look into the mirror
And this is what I see
Only one reflection remains
And that reflection is me

I am the first
The second could
Never be set free

The Storm

Like a thunderstorm he comes
Fast a furious
Darkness he brings
His voice like thunder
Loud and crashing
Each word hits like the lightening
Striking through the heart
Tears falling with the rain
And then the storm is over
As fast as it came
Damage left behind
Is all the storm has left
Just like the words upon my mind'
This storm is over until the next time

Razorblade 2-Scars

Some may think its all in the mind
But unless you've lived it
You will never quite know
What makes the addiction grow

You try to hide it
But the scars they show
You want someone to understand
This is not something that is planned.

It's a release, of pain and anger,
You've held deep inside,
And you cut when you've lost all
Your pride.

Scars are the telltale sign,
Of someone struggling with the pain
In their mind.

It could be the angry words
You say
That I hold inside that makes me
Feel that way.

Holding the razorblade against my skin
Struggling with the pain held within.

Just one cut can take away the pain
I tell myself it will keep me from
going insane.

Just one cut is all I need,
Just one cut,
I watch as I bleed.

Each cut deeper than the one before
I watch as the blood flows freely upon
the floor.

Scars are the telltale sign
Of someone struggling with the pain
in their mind.

How long will this last
Until it is finally over?

I'm tired of the scars inside and out
I wish I could stop this without a doubt.

Will the razorblade be my friend?
I hope I don't find out.

By dying in the end.

Memories of My Past

Life once had meaning,
And it was then I was safe.
I once felt free,
Just to be me.

I once had a smile,
Upon my face.
Now this all has been erased.

To many times you've put me down,
Made my tears flow upon the ground.

Smiling is something I used to do,
But you took that away,
With each word you had to say.

Now I walk in silence,
With a heart of stone.
All my friends are gone,

You've left me all alone.
Is this how your Love is shown?

Questions

How do you stop the pain you feel from taking over your life?
How do stop the control of another from taking you down?
How do you stop the fear you feel inside?
These are the questions I ask myself each and every day,
Should I run away or should I stay?
Maybe it'll be better.
Maybe it'll be worse.
Maybe if I leave he'll follow me,
And end my questions before I have the answer.

Brick Wall

Brick by brick,
I built this wall,
I try to climb up,
But still I fall

Behind this wall,
You will see,
The one who I am,
And not that you want me to be.

I put on a mask,
To hide my face,
Behind this wall,
Is my hiding place.

I can't knock it down,
It's built to strong,
I try to climb out,
But still I fall.

I guess my place,
Is behind this wall.

Hiding from you,
And hiding from me.
Brick by brick.

Now I Lay Me Down to Sleep

A cut so deep for never ending pain,
A stream of blood runs down the drain,
The razorblade becomes my friend,
Will I die in the end?

I cut and cut and all I do is bleed,
But the pain I am feeling never really
recedes.

Tears they may fall,
But there's really no feeling left at all,
Inside I'm dying,
Do you hear me crying?

I cut for a peace,
A peace within,
Please don't cry,

Hurting inside sometimes its hard to hide,
But no one can say I haven't tried.

Darkness comes,
I search for the light,

I think it's time to just give up the fight.
A cut to deep,
Now I lay me down to sleep.

Razorblade—The End

Ripping and tearing upon my skin,
Aching to release the pain within,
Zig zag cut along my face,
Over my body and down to the waist,
Releasing pain in a hope for peace,
Bloody nightmare will never cease,
Leaving nothing left untouched,
Another cut I watch the blood gush,
Dripping slowly I collapse to the floor,
Eternally bleeding no more.

Scars

Signs of the pain,
Cutting brings,
Addicting cuts,
Ripped apart and sewn shut,
Signature of one who cuts.

Pain

Pulsating throughout,
Aching no doubt,
Intensified inside,
Numb.

Pain it can drain,
Drive you insane,
Mess with your brain.

Innocence Taken

A little girl of 8 years old,
Her innocence taken on a night so cold.
As she sleeps,
In he creeps.
As she feels his weight,
She awakes.

All she can see is his face.
She tries to scream.
She tries to shout.
But she's so scared,
nothing comes out.

He holds her down.
He enters her.
She screams in pain.
Innocence taken from one so young.

In her mind,
She wonders what she has done.

She's fighting back.
She wants to run.
It's over now he is done.

With a smile on his face,
He looks at her.
Says don't tell anyone.

It's was suppose to be fun.
He leaves the room.
She curls in a ball.
This wasn't fun to me;
It wasn't fun at all.
Now she holds this secret within,
About the horrible night,
Her innocence was taken.

Beneath the Willow Tree

Below the branches of the willow tree,
She sat alone;
She didn't want to be.

She cried out for help but no one was there.
No one cared;
Would this life be spared?

Below the branches of the willow tree,
Her empty heart cried;
But no one to see.

All she wants is to be set free,
Her smile fake;
Not what you see.

Below the branches of the willow tree,
Screaming inside,
All alone and on her own.

Anger fills her deep inside;
Lost all reason to try,
She tries to hold on,
But feels her life is gone.

Her life in chains;
Herself she blames.
Below the branches of the willow tree,
Her empty heart cries.
Here but not alive;
This her last goodbye.

He Thinks He's Just a Friend

To have feelings for someone so deep,
That your voice cannot speak.

You want to tell him how you feel;
That what you feel for him is real.

But maybe what you feel for him,
Is not felt back the same,
Maybe someone else calls his name.

My heart breaks,
For another's heart he aches,
But its my heart that he takes.

Tears I cry,
He will never know why.

He thinks he's just a friend.
How can I tell him its much more.
Should I walk away?
Or open up the door?

If I tell him how I feel,
That what I feel for him is real,
Will he understand,
Or does his heart have other plans?

Will he run away?
Or can his heart,
Be mine someday?

For this is what I pray,
So my friend,
What do you say?

Can your heart,
Be mine,
Or will you run away?

Maybe someday you'll read this,
And answer with a kiss,
For its your heart that I wish.

He thinks he's just a friend,
Is that where it will end?

Etched by Scars

Eyes of brown,
In crimson blood they drown.

Etched by scars,
So precise,
The razorblade cuts,
Deeper than the knife,
End of hope,
With every cut,
And slice.

Complete emptiness,
Silent my tears,
Razors edge,
The end is near.

Faces hide as much as they reveal,
Imprisioned in this life,
Pain forever sealed.

I cut for everything,
For not being enough,
From the inside looking out,

This night my last,
There is no doubt.

Don't try to save me,
I just want to be free,
No one will ever know,
For no one tried to see,
The person inside,
That always cried.

In a different time,
In a different place,
Maybe my life,
Wouldn't of been erased.

Please don't judge,
Unless you know,
Why I cut,
Why my pain,
I never let show.

Hoping not to survive this night.
No more fear.
No more fight.
With this cut,
My
Last
Goodnight.

I Am

I am blind.
I cannot see.
Dreams for me,
Can never be.

I am deaf.
I cannot hear.
Your voice of anger
Has been erased.

Mouth sewn shut.
I cannot talk.
For words I say
Matter not.

Heart of stone,
Cannot be broke,
No love to feel,
For love is not real.

Nothing left of me inside.
I'm not a slave.
I no longer will hide.

I stand alone.
No feelings will I have shown.
For all is gone now,
Right down to the bone,

Chains around my neck,
I was just your pet.

Now that I am dead,
My blood you can no longer shed.

Are You Ready

Would you be ready if he came today?
Did you try to follow in his ways?
Did you remember to give him praise,
As you knelt and prayed…

Did you remember to thank him for all that he has made?

Did you try to follow in his light?
And always try to do what was right…
Would you be worthy in his sight?
If you're not ready,
You can always start tonight.
Don't wait till it's to late….
As soon you may be at Heaven's gate…
There is always time to get your life straight…

Angels Cry

A single raindrop falls to the ground.
Down came more, barely making a sound.

As I turn and look around
A thought came to me so profound.

Maybe teardrops are what I see
Falling from the sky.

And so I start to wonder why
What has made the angels cry,
From their clouds so high

Could it be we were not listening
When the Lord came whispering

That made the angels cry their tears
That fell like rain from the sky.

Guide Me

I haven't found my way yet,
I wonder if I ever will,
In this darkness,
I struggle to search for the light,
Forgive me for being weak,
Its only you that I seek,
I pray for strength and guidance,
To fill my mind with silence,
To wash away my tears,
To rid me of my fears
Take my hand and guide me,
Help me to see,
As I get on my knees,
In prayer,
I know that you are always there.

Our Guide

When hope is growing dim
And it seems as though you can't win
Remember to put your trust in Him

Let the light of the Lord guide you
In all you're going through

Let Him guide your footsteps
In everything you do

And when your faith falters
And hope seems far away

Remember the Lord is with you
All you have to do is pray

For he is always listening
Waiting for your whisperings

So don't be led astray
For he waits for you today

Get upon your knees and pray
And in faith say the things
You need to say

Remember He is with you
And that the power of the
Holy Spirit is greater than
Any task you face

If I Had Only Given My All

The pain and suffering I could no longer bear
I prayed please take me from here

You sent me Angels in the way of friends
To show me the way back, to make amends

My faith renewed, as I knelt in prayer
A quiet moment, all doubt swept away,
I felt your presence, as I prayed today

As my tears fell, I knew I'd found my way
The sad thing is, I could have bypassed the fall
If I had only given you my all.

Take It to the Lord in Prayer

Take it to the Lord in prayer,
For he is always there,
He knows your every care,
No matter what trials you,
may bare.

Take it to the Lord in prayer,
No matter the time or where,
He awaits your prayers,
Get down upon your knees,
and share,
Your testimony to others bare,

Take it to the Lord in prayer.

Heaven's Gate

Its to late,
When standing at heavens gate,
To change the words of hate,
Those words of hate,
Were the devils bait,
And now its to late to set things straight.

Now you stand before him,
Knowing of your sins.

To have followed in his light,
To of strived to choose the right,
Then you really might,
Have won the fight,
If you would of just held to his words real tight.

If only you had followed his plan,
And did not choose to bury your head in the sand,
Your reward would of been grand.

And now you stand at heavens gate,
Wishing you could change your fate,
And knowing now that it is to late.

In Another Place

In another place,
Left without a trace,
No longer to live in disgrace,
No more sadness upon my face.

Do not look for me,
For I'm not there you see,
I'm in a place where I can be me,
Where I have wings to fly free.

Soaring high into the sky,
No more will I have to cry,
The pain and hurt you applied,
Went away when I died.

I can be happy here,
In this place I no longer have fear,
And my mind is now clear,
Full of light, love and cheer.

I pray someday from your anger you
will flee,
And grow some wings and be set free,
To fly in the sky with me.

Thank You Friend

Thank You Friend
The past has left its mark on you
And many times you've cried
For fallen soldiers and many friends have died
When I think of you my heart is filled with pride
I'm here for you
You're not alone
A friend is by your side
When your sad or feeling blue
My heart with you resides
I cannot fix your broken heart
Nor take away your pain
All I can do
Is be there for you
When things are feeling dark
I only hope the words I've wrote
Have left a mark upon your heart.

Wings of an Angel

Always watching
Never judge
Gentle whispers
Elegant spirit
Listening always
Shimmering light.
Wings of an Angel
Felt but not seen,
Feels like a dream,
Wings of an Angel in flight,
What a beautiful sight,
Watching day and night.
I don't have to see my Angel,
To know that he is there,
It's a feeling inside my heart,
Something felt in the air.
When I call I know that he'll appear,
To wipe away my tears,
And free me of my fears.
My Angel walks with me everyday,
I wouldn't want it any other way.

Life of Failure

No one is human,
When all we do is,
Tear each others hearts apart.

We are no better than another of this world,
We are all just monsters,
Here to live in eternal life of hate and destruction,
Beyond this life of failure.

by Amber Vorthmann

The Secret

To love someone and not be able to let it show,
To have to hide your feelings and not let them know.

If he only knew how she truly feels,
Maybe it would make a difference, maybe it could be real,
For I know her heart he steals.

She says she cannot tell him this,
For another he can't resist,
For her this love, she will miss.

Her heart broken in two,
And he will never have a clue,
Or even a chance to undo.

She says she's alright,
But I hear her crying in the night.

She thinks no one can hear,
But I can feel her pain loud and clear,
For she is my mother dear,
For her I will always be near.

I Love You Mom,
I know you will be strong.

Broken Angel

One wing fell to the ground,
Then the other both without making a sound,
All alone no one around,
Wearing a smile to hide the frown,
This Angels wings have fallen down.

Once she flew high into the sky,
Now this broken angel cries,
Tears like rain from her eyes,
Do you even wonder why?
Shes given up no longer to fly.
She use to dream,
Now only screams,
Nothing left for her it seems.

Broken Angel sits and cries,
Heart is broken inside,
This she tries to hide.

Broken Angel lost her wings,
Nothing left for her to dream.

Lost Love

Once I gave myself to a very special man
I thought we'd be together forever
That was my plan
He was my soul mate
We were meant to be
Or so I thought
But the joke was on me
I gave him my heart right from the start
We had a connection so strong
A very special bond
I thought we'd never part
A past life for him came along
I let him go to hold him would be wrong
You can't hold someone's heart
When to another it belongs
I thought he loved me
But you see
I was wrong.

Sick and Tired

Always sick and always tired
But life goes on like nothing is wrong
Test after test and nothing is found
Will it be to late when they finally see?
That there is something wrong with me.

And so I go on day to day
And hope that whatever it is will go away,
I try to pretend I'm feeling fine,
Put on a smile to hide how I feel,
And try to make believe the pain isn't
real.

Maybe someday they will figure it out,
And find I was really sick,
Without a doubt.

My Friend Randy

I am a flower and you my stem,
Held together for all time.

I am but a cloud and you my sky,
With you around I never have to wonder why.

I am a willow,
And you my branches.
Held together forever.

I am but a butterfly,
And you my wings,
As we soar through the sky,
All our dreams can be seen.

I am a boat,
And you my sail,
Drifting along in peace,
Sharing our dreams.

I am but me,
And you are you,
We have a friendship ever so true.

Never forget me,
As I shall never forget you,

Our bridge is friendship,
Held together with glue.

My friend Randy,
Always remember I will always,
Be here for you.

My Friend

IM's we exchange,
Some may think it strange,
But it's something I wouldn't change.

You seem to know just what to say,
You've touched my heart in a special way,
You've helped me believe things will be ok.

You have helped me face my fears,
And wipe away some of the tears,
That hasn't happen in many a year.

You have made me smile,
Something I haven't done in a while.

I have found a friend in you,
A friend I know is true,
That friend is you.

Thank you Gary for just being you.

Rodeo

Bull and rider at the ready,
Hand wrapped in rope,
To hold the cowboy steady.

The gate is released,
The bull bolts out,
A strong muscular beast.

A cowboy out to prove,
He can ride this bull,
He will not be removed.

An 8 second ride is all it takes,
But there is no room for mistakes.

The buzzer sounds,
He's made the ride,
In this small town,
His heart is filled with pride.

The crowd cheers for a good ride,
The cowboy kneels down,
Kisses the ground,
And thanks God for being by his side,
And getting him safely through his ride.

Shady

You write about cutting and dying inside,
How life hurts and how you want to hide.

How can I make you understand?
You have a friend by your side,
That will be with you for the long ride.

I don't want to judge you,
I'm here to be your friend,
Thats what friends are to do.

I want you to know,
That no matter what you do,
And how you decide to let your feelings show.

I will always be right there by your side,
Helping you through the anger and hurt,
So don't feel like you have to hide,

I've been there to and I have cried,
For a life full of pain and hurt deep inside.

Remember Shady,
I am here for you,

You can call on me,
And you will see,
You'll always have a friend in me.

Behind the Wall

Built a wall,
You can't get in,
Kick it, push it,
It won't fall.

You cannot get through,
My solid wall.

You cannot hurt me anymore,
Your words do penetrate,
Not even the floor.

I cannot feel your hate,
Behind the wall I did create.

Keep trying if you will,
No more my soul,
For you to steal.

I Built this wall,
To never fall,
No lock, no key,

You can never,
Get to me.

Behind my wall,
I am safe,
From your call.

Built a wall,
Can't you see,
Behind my wall,
You can never be.

Darkness

I am darkness,
I cover the night,
I bring fear,
Into the hearts of many,
Lost souls,
Are mine to take,
I am a nightmare,
Only you're awake,
I am hate,
Come meet your fate,
For
You
I
Wait.

Nothing

You can't hurt me,
I do not feel,
I am nothing you see,
Nothing is what is,
Left of me.

I cry no tears,
I have no fears.

Nothing is what,
I've become through out the years.

I am here,
But not even seen,
I am hidden,
Gone like the air,
Invisible to you,
And to me,
I am nothing,
Not even a dream.

I am nothing,
Sad thing is,
I don't even care.
Nothing "Poof"!!
Not
There.

What I Wanted

I live in reality,
But what I wanted,
Was only pretend.

What I wanted was a dream,
But what I got was nothing.

What you wanted you got,
What I wanted I lost.

You got happy,
I got hurt.

You reached for the stars,
And left me with,
Nothing but scars.

What I wanted,
Was to scream your name,
What I got,
Was to find,
You didn't feel the same.

What I wanted,
Oh just forget it,
Doesn't matter anyway.

Control

Sit upon your throne,
My life is not my own.

Chained and shackled,
Put in my place,
Made to feel,
Like a disgrace.

Control everything I do,
I have no friends,
You scared them away,

An animal in a cage,
Only you hold the key,
You threw it away,
So I can never be free.

Locked up forever,
My life you hold,

This is how it's supposed to be,
Or so I've been told.

Said You Loved Me

Said you loved me,
But you lied.

Said you loved me,
But made me cry.

Said you loved me,
You never even tried.

Said you loved me,
But you hurt me inside.

Said you loved me,
But love is not the,
Taking of pride.

Said you loved me,
But that has died.

Always in the Way

Nothing good to say,
Always in the way,
Only work never play,

Hoping there will come a day,
When in the bed you made you shall lay,
No one more for your prey.

This is my hope and my prayer,
That someday you will see your error,
That you will finally care,
For someone other than yourself.

Perfect

A perfect wife,
Perfect kids,
Perfect house,
Who lives like this?

Everything done just your way,
No talking back,
As we have no say.

Chained to this house,
No where to go,
This is how you keep control.

Everything clean,
Done just right,
But not for you,
You start a fight.
Up all night,
Trying to get it just right.

You say that nothing is done,
Even though we worked,
Until we saw the sun.

A perfect wife,
And perfect kids,

A perfect house,
"Please Lord,"
Help us to get out!!

Web of Deceit

Wrapped up in a web,
Trapped am I,
Like the spider,
Traps the fly.

A web of rejection,
Spun from deception,
No offer of protection.

The prey that you seek,
That you have made weak,
Caught in a web of your deceit,
Something I'd rather not repeat.

The harder I struggle to be released,
The stronger your hold,
And now you dissect me piece by piece.

The Brown Bear

Bear of brown,
Went to town,
Wearing a crown,
He found on the ground,
He had a frown,
When he heard a loud sound,
It came from the pound,
The sound was from a hound,
Bear turned around,
And homeward he was bound.

by Misti Ostby

Deer

I saw a deer,
With one big ear,
I saw it from my,
Rear view mirror.

As it came near,
You could see its fear,
A noise I did hear.

As another car steered clear,
Trying not to hit the deer.

by Misti Ostby

Tick the Chick

I had a chick,
His name I did pick,
I called him Tick.

He liked to peck and kick at sticks,
He thought it was a neat lil trick,
If he had a tongue,
I'd teach him to lick.

by Misti Ostby

A Cat Named Pat

There was a cat,
His name was Pat,
He wore a red hat,

As he sat on his mat,
His tummy was getting fat,
From eating a big rat,
What do you think of that?

by Misti Ostby

Drowning in My Sorrow

Drowning in my sorrow,
Bleeding through my pain,
Its like you stuck a knife in me,
And left me here to drain.

Every time I look at you,
My heart is filled with pain,
I can't even be near you,
Or I will go insane.

You are like a freight train,
You ran over my heart,
And crushed everything,
Nothing will ever be the same,
And your the one I blame.

by Paige Vorthmann

Only Life I Know

Give up! Quiet! You're beaten!
Is all you have to say,
Why does it always have to be this way?

Failure is all I am to you,
No matter what I do,
And I never know what I've done,
I don't have a clue.

As I hang my head in shame,
I know that again I'm the blame,
For what I do not know,
I guess because I let my feelings show.

I try to stand up to you every now and then,
Only to be knocked down again.

And so I just pretend,
That everything is great,

But in my heart I am feeling hate.
Please rescue me before it becomes to late,

Must this be my life?
Is this to be my fate?

My head hung low,
No feelings do I show,
This is the only life I know.

As You Sleep

So long have I cried,
While you lay there by my side.

You never even know,
Because no feelings do I show.

Feelings are not allowed,
Of this you seem to be proud.

I've tried to run away,
But you made me stay,
You watched me as if I was your prey.

Locked in chains,
As you control my brain,
Driving me insane,
Always the one you blame.

As you sleep,
I try to hide,
But you always seek,
And again take me to your side.

No way out,
I scream and shout,
Of this there is no doubt.

Let me be,
Set me free,
This I hope to someday see.

To Take a Stand

To take a Stand,
This is my Plan,
No longer to bury my head in the sand.

You will not hurt me anymore,
This is the final score,
No longer will my feelings be tore.

I've always tried to live this way,
"I've heard the hurtful things you'd say",
This game, I'll no longer play.

I let you knock me down,
Turn a smile into a frown;
I will no longer be your clown,
For you to boss around.

I Love you still this is true,
But I can no longer live this way with you.

Will You

Would you be there if I were to call?
Will you pick me up when I fall,
Or do I have to write my name on the wall,
For you to notice me at all.

I seem invisible to you,
Unless there's something,
You want me to do,
You know the words I speak are true.

You've already lost me,
Yet you don't even know.

We don't even talk anymore,
Maybe your to busy,
With one of your whore's.

Will you realize before it to late?
Or will you wait till there is nothing,
but hate?

Someone for Me

Will there ever be,
Someone for me?

Someone who will care,
Someone to share,
Someone who will be there.

Someone who will hold my hand,
Someone who with me will stand.

Someone that will treat me right,
Someone that just doesn't want a fight,
Someone who will hold me tight.

Will there ever be,
Someone
For
Me?

To Make a Change

I threw away my razor today,
No longer will I use it to take the pain away.

Although it feels a little strange,
I knew I had to make a change.

Cutting never really solved anything,
Just a lot more problems it did bring.

Now left with the scars today,
I have learned it did not take the hurt away.

I hope if you do this you will know,
That your pain never really goes,
When you cut and watch the blood flow,
And you just end up feeling low.

I hope that someday you will see,
And make a change just like me,
And from the guilt you will be set free.

Thin Strands

Use to hold her heart in his hands,
Now nothings left but thin strands,
Maybe that was your plan.

Words said in anger you can never take back,
This I can tell you is a fact,
Wisdom you seem to lack,
Life going down the wrong track.

Heart broken in two,
Torn into pieces by you,
Nothing left for you to do.

Leaving today,
Nothing standing in the way,
For a new life she prays.

Use to hold her heart in his hands,
Now nothing left but thin strands.

Band-Aid on Your Feelings

I wish you could put a band-aid on your feelings,
But that's not the way it works,
Although you are in pain,
And it really hurts.

A band-aid does not bend a broken heart,
Or angry words that have tore your world apart.

With a band-aid you can cover a wounded knee,
But you can't cover your feelings as you can see,
Wouldn't it be nice if a band-aid could do this for thee?

I wish you could put a band-aid on your feelings,
That would be great,
If only a band-aid could cover up the words said in hate.

I wish you could put a band-aid on your feelings.

But you can't!!